All you have to do is ask

ANHINGA PRESS

All you have to do is ask

MEREDITH WALTERS

2006 ANHINGA PRIZE FOR POETRY
SELECTED BY SIDNEY WADE

ANHINGA PRESS
TALLAHASSEE, FLORIDA
2007

Cover art: Louise Lawler, *Portrait*, 1982,
        Cibachrome, 19 x 19 inches
        Courtesy of the Artist and Metro Pictures
Author photo: Marjorie Zapruder
Cover design, book design, and production: C. L. Knight
Typesetting: C.L. Knight
Type Styles: titles and text set in Palatino Linotype

Library of Congress Cataloging-in-Publication Data
All you have to do is ask by Meredith Walters – First Edition
ISBN – 978-0-938078-97-5
Library of Congress Cataloging Card Number – 2007928077

This publication is sponsored in part by a grant
from the Florida Department of State,
Division of Cultural Affairs, and the Florida Arts Council.

Anhinga Press Inc. is a nonprofit corporation dedicated wholly to the
publication and appreciation of fine poetry and other literary genres.

For personal orders, catalogs
and information write to:
Anhinga Press
P.O. Box 10595
Tallahassee, Florida 32302
Web site: www.anhinga.org
E-mail: info@anhinga.org

Published in the United States
by Anhinga Press
Tallahassee, Florida
First Edition, 2007

For Sarah Josephine and Michelle

CONTENTS

ix   *Acknowledgments*

5   The Scribe's Umbrella

8   It is Interesting and Difficult Work, Ladies

9   Hum of Little Engines and Palm-sized Devices

10   Thanks Again for What You Said about My Aura

11   Telegrams for New Doctrine Smith

13   Your Name Written on a Grain of Rice

14   Love Note to a Young Soldier

16   How to Tell if You've Been Reincarnated

17   Poem Transcribed to the Path Smoke Takes

19   And By Way of Example She Points to the Sun

21   Robert Creeley Boards the S.S. John F. Kennedy

23   Bridal Veil Falls

24   Brief Hist. of Contemp. Art

25   Oh Stars

26   Blue Coat Beside a Black Jacket

27   This Poem Happens in Spring

28   Faux Tough

29   Why I Long to Be a Pine Tree: Godzilla's Haiku Journey

32   The Army of God Strikes Camp in Utah

33   Your Name Written on a Grain of Rice II

34   What Shall I Take of What I Need?

35   Seaweed Theory

37   Forces Suspected but Never Observed

38   The First Time I Saw the Rio Grande
       I Could Only Think of Marty Robbins

39   Virgins Who Speak in Riddles Will Not Stay Virgins Long

40   Common Dream Birds

42   Li Po Made Me Think

43   Penny Arcade Portrait of Lauren Bacall

44   What Things Declare

45   No One Can Always Ever Predict Correctly the Weather

47   Lines Whispered into a Teacup

48   Spontaneous Monument

50   All You Have to Do is Ask

53   Notes

55   About the Author

ACKNOWLEDGMENTS

"Why I Long to Be a Pine Tree: Godzilla's Haiku Journey" and "The First Time I Saw the Rio Grande I Could Only Think of Marty Robbins" appeared in *Spout.*

"The Army of God Strikes Camp in Utah" appeared in *Conduit.*

"Spontaneous Monument" appeared in *Isn't It Romantic: 100 Love Poems by Younger American Poets,* Verse Press 2004.

"Forces Suspected but Never Observed," "This Poem Happens in Spring," "Blue Coat Beside a Black Jacket," "Brief Hist. of Contemp. Art," "How to Tell if You've Been Reincarnated," and "Your Name Written on a Grain of Rice" appeared in *Subtropics.*

I would like to thank Bill Waltz and John Colburn for publishing some of my poems in their journals *Conduit* and *Spout;* Matt Hunter, Barb Elam, John Vogt, Donna Gunderson for their support; Sean and Finn; Jane Miller and David Shapiro; MJZ for inspiring me to start writing again; Sidney Wade for taking notice; and Lynne Knight and Rick Campbell for their hard work.

it is a privilege to see so
much confusion. Disguised by what
might seem the opposite ...
     — Marianne Moore, *The Steeple-Jack*

Come body! Come life!
Come to me
double stem of columbine with your signature semantics.
Come record player,
cicada with microbanjo,
question that decides to shake me,
tremulous father, doorway.

THE SCRIBE'S UMBRELLA

In such a season as recalls the sun, an ashtray full of pennies,
a visit to a widow leads you to wonder:
virtue and integrity, the effort to be a great man
among bouts of neuralgia, neurosis,
the rum someone slipped in your soda
for which you do not remember asking,
to take suitable decisions —
where is it true to say you live, when lions pace elsewhere, terrific
and recalled from memory? A river of wine, a river of honey,
a river that sings: do not ask what is suffered elsewhere.
A bridge over the river to the Bronx.

In such a season,
two kids in a sort of strange song and dance in the vestibule
of their mother's bank lead you to wonder
how a tune might begin that praises a widow
who never touches her dead husband's books. A sculpture
unearthed again depicts a scribe with his case and absent stylus
but does not mete the hours that passed from task to task.
What sign to make among disbelievers? You have been called
by a singer unseen and such is your nature
that even the spaces between questions call to you.

An apocryphal lion roams the Venetian landscape.
It roams St. Petersburg, it roams the Bronx.
Your advisors, despite the distance of an era awaiting
excavation, only suggest what it might be like
to leave and not to abandon yourself.
Apprentice the hands to the violin
to forge a memory, to strike a path, to be your passage
from uncertainty, like building a wing
on a building.

In such a season as a woman in furs puts her poodle in a cab
the scribe amends the story to end:
"And they were terrified."
The effortless gesture, the trained arm, the hand is a voice,
the hand enthroned.
Fear and fearfulness. What you know to be
your left ventricle, where a violin awaits the accompaniment
of a provisional composition, as compassion —
what is suffered elsewhere.
What the river is like, what the war is like, what doubt is like.
The bravery to say happiness in a dark age.
We are merciless in our regrets.

Thought and thinking.
A table of friends who do not know where to begin
their renditions of all they fear they allowed to let pass.
The time spent thinking, time wasted being afraid,
knowing and responsibility, idea and mind,
thought and unknown, an actual umbrella.
Friend, have you too been abandoned?
And if so by what?

Should you, a scribe among contemporaries record them
as heroes of mystical texts?
Their fingers aren't god.
The great permissions, the great restraints. First the songs,
then the theories.
You recover your questions:
How can the water of a lake be both clear and blue?
Have you dreamt the white flag?
To make distinctions in darkness.
A song whose only words are every way to say no.
An involuntary memory.

6

You praise the clear darkness.
To say no to every question is triumphant.

A great man once said, "Fresh Kills is a collage."
A great man once said, "The mind is a mechanized Atlantic."
To call on the widow of a great man,
to be an apprentice, a scribe, to be a great man,
to be unable.
How you are seen by someone with your back toward her
in a bath of sunlight
you would be too shy to accept should you realize its presence.
And instead you turn your son's attention to his shadow.

When the widow utters instructions for surviving a war
and likens death to bread thrown into the sea,
you understand that you do not yet know.
When your god waves from a bridge
from which he will not be talked down, the sky unravels
into a forged Venetian twilight
where you recover first one idea, then another.
The river shall gather its skirts and journey across the lion.
You are forgiven.

IT IS INTERESTING
AND DIFFICULT WORK, LADIES

Incubator, I am weak with knowing hunger. A tiny bulb warms me.
Tungsten stem, tungsten tongue in a hot little head —
twee twee!
I am a bald egg, little egg shaking in the wind
where my tree should be.
A meager bed of straw is standard issue twilight.
It is upon me: the real one with stars
and a snail of moon.
I have heard about the sea and think I belong there.
Twee twee, I've been lying this whole time.
I am not an egg but I have an egg for a body, guess what:
I am an octopus
propelled by bellows pelagic. This pigment
I instinctively muster for I am full of mistrust
turns me to coral or an angry white.
I appear in the field notes of a certain French biologist
whom I came to love
for his homeostatic genius and all the eggs he fed me.
I now know that I will never be a wife.

HUM OF LITTLE ENGINES
AND PALM-SIZED DEVICES

Nothing big happens
amid deforestation and superlative white sales.
The refrigerator develops a nasty buzz,
Washington runs a bad play against Miami,
and I stand like a poodle
in a construction zone, unable to name what is missing.
Fearfulness moves me,
like you, unseeingly toward the car door.
My journeys tend to end in grief
among racks of clearance sweaters,
where I suddenly lament the steady loss of the manatee.
I owe an apology to any of several words
denoting any of several American larches.
I have no excuse except to say that I have no religion,
the nightjar's cries do not resemble mine.
In my willingness to remain a stranger to the trees I pass
I keep as a secret my search for one ecstatic welcome.
My chambered heart echoes dragonfly geometry, but I do not know
what it intends, I cannot name the cause or consequence.
What's the voice of Maria Callas to sparrows in warehouse rafters?
Strangely, under the streets,
Tuvan throat singers offer a chorus in praise of war ponies.
Yes, like me.

THANKS AGAIN FOR WHAT
YOU SAID ABOUT MY AURA

To be as the honeysuckle, a draped adornment of the helioscape
Cynthia wears her wooden necklace
priestess-wise and it calls my eyes toward her deeply trying
to accept her place among us — death's mark.
When she clings to the fence and speaks of going
"into the light for a while," I envision a middle-distance picture
of a lone figure shape-shifting into flame.
If someone took a photo of us right now, casual stances
and t-shirts, they could create for her a halo from available light,
as though the shutter captured the moment
of her transubstantiation.
But where would you keep a picture like that?
And in fact, forget the halo, make sure you get her face
for she is inexplicably in eye shadow
to tend her gladiolas.
Because I am an Aquarius I am like an underground river
she tells me, and further I am confused and heart-addled
because Saturn has returned for me
as it will again in thirty years
for we are transfigured despite our will by forces
so astronomic, so astrological
as to become illegible to ourselves.
A smudge for some, for others a fire.

TELEGRAMS FOR NEW DOCTRINE SMITH

1
I belong to nothing
but the trees I remember,
the seeds that cling to my socks,
the people with coats like me.

2
Alone, you are as we are, arranging the pantry,
half-listening to the radio news from your neighbor's house:
Women and children, abandoned by spring,
sell the dinner table and hit the road.

3
We sent the eldest ahead for some kind of word.
Now they are all MCs. They name-check you in their rhymes.
They are no longer ours. They are underdressed
and assemble secretly.

4
The view of the river, the river itself.
There are many ways of being.

5
Where once we sang our poems by heart,
you will find us window shopping among strangers
with no memory of our names.

6
The tourists are ruining Angkor Wat but the locals need money.
Is there a god of money?
Is he a citizen of another dimension?
Conceive of his residence in order to conceive of him.

7
A Coney Island Renaissance
threatens the entire Atlantic Seaboard.
We wander beaches to look for prizes from the Eisenhower
administration. Sneakers from the shipwreck: our mates
will come ashore on an unmanned archipelago.

YOUR NAME WRITTEN ON A GRAIN OF RICE

Every grain of sand
multiplied by the number of galaxies in the observable universe
equals all the starfish stranded on a shore, where a single soul
throws back as many as he can
despite the defeatist ridicule of a passerby.
This story is supposed to be an inspirational device.
My mother won the Star-Thrower Award
for her outstanding customer service and afterwards
she could turn "mistakes" into "teachable moments"
and would substitute the word "problem"
with the word "challenge."
After a CCD screening of *Our Lady of Fatima,*
Sister Immaculata asked me if I wanted to be an angel when I died,
and I replied that I'd rather be an asteroid belt.
She said that she would pray for me, except for the word "pray"
substitute "break your spirit with New Testament Coloring Books."
Then Anna McClintock died.
"God called her back to heaven," the Sister told me,
which left open the possibility that I could call her back down here,
but they buried her, beloved daughter and sister, on a vast lawn
and marked her spot with a stone lamb,
even though she was more dolphin than lamb.

LOVE NOTE TO A YOUNG SOLDIER

No one around me seems to care about the view, which is the same
on both sides of the plane — the cities burn themselves
through the clouds: Washington is a gaudy earring.
Norfolk fluoresces, a jellyfish.

I'm going to take it as a sign.
Because it's pretty and it seems like a sign. Maybe it means
even if there isn't a God at least there is a world
where people can fly at their leisure.
My captain is flying me closer to the moon
than the clouds get to be tonight. All I had to do was pay
and now I am oceans of air above Atlanta next to you,
Second Lieutenant Rodriguez.

You who gave up this view for an aisle seat.
Ever since we climbed to cruising altitude you've been gazing
at the same sexy gin ad, ordering straight tonic from the cart.
Maybe you're trying to ignore the woman in F3 who's talking
way too loud about her pugs between sips of zinfandel, then waving
three singles in the air, her fingers covered in gold rings.

But you're young and all potential, and killing yourself
by denying pure whimsy.
I want to cross the aisle and whisper: "Would you mind
if I told you we were closer to the moon than the clouds?"
But you might take it as a come-on.
Or think that my timing was bad,
or that I had no right to interrupt your thoughts.
Like I was tapping your phone line.

And you're right. Who'm I to you? What's it to me?
It's the clouds and the buildings below them
twinkling in well-planned grids.
It's the exhilaration of knowing there are greater forces
determining the most efficient traffic patterns
and planning covenants
with their own communities. Certain codes should not be broken.

All passengers can have as many little pretzels as they want
and meanwhile the earth sprawls under us
a starlet, all glittery and smoky and you, young soldier,
hover above her. She is available to the eye all at once
while you dream of gin you shouldn't drink in uniform.
As if nothing existed beyond your desire or your duty to thwart
threats both foreign and domestic.
Who would it kill for you to loosen up a bit?

What would it take? A dirty joke? Someone wanting to know where
you're from? Unbuckle yourself and come back to the window,
fill your eyes with these lights.
I close my eyes and see you standing guard
along a stretch of chain link, nothing around but echo
and unrecognizable space, the black bags of meals-ready-to-eat.

You have one hour. Look out the window and pretend
you are in command of everything.
Order a drink. You are so high, so safe, and if you take off your pin,
no one will know your name.

HOW TO TELL IF YOU'VE BEEN REINCARNATED

The generals McClellan, Patton, and Eisenhower,
at ease in the privations and triumphs of war
each concluded that he was the reincarnation
of Napoleon Bonaparte.
Believing that you are Napoleon is not the same
as having a Napoleon complex, because if you are Napoleon
you can't be like Napoleon.
Napoleon thought of himself as a modern Alexander the Great
but Alexander, as far as we know,
was never bitten on the ass by his wife's Bichon Frise,
nor did he ever execute a Bichon Frise.

Sir Edmund Hillary defied death when he scaled Mount Everest
with his fearless friend, the Sherpa
Tensing Norgay.
Years later in an under-reported adventure
the duo embarked on a search for the Abominable Snowman,
which is the same thing as a Yeti.
They hunted through fearsome illness
and bouts of Shelley for that lone human-animal,
at home in devastating ice and altitude.
They found nothing except a blue crevasse,
the kind that emits sublime
and unending howls.
This they could neither conquer nor honor.

POEM TRANSCRIBED TO THE PATH SMOKE TAKES

every busy signal and its destination
every hand waving toward a more-distant traveler
each sleep-evaded insomniac in every wakeful bed
every tongue, word or whistle
every whistle leaving through an open window
every car alarm
every mispronounced name
every thigh, the arches of all feet
all daydreams of unchosen lovers
every mistake, every grievance unuttered
every fallen horse, soldier, believer, criminal
every released fish swimming sideways
all disarmed naysayers
every misconceived idea
every traveler, effort and journey
all unheard hellos, every mumbled curse
every crow eating from a To-Go box
every stayed hand
each watch fire on a farther plateau
every asshole you ever met
every punch in the face
each mind in pain
each leafless elm
all spaces between tree branches and the eyes that record them
each grapefruit, each tendon, each ruby
every child army
each coiled rat snake, deer skull, celestial plexus
any of the smaller mysteries
the wordless questions
the disbelievers
the cartographers

each mummy in a vitrine
galaxy necklaced by dust
anything with breath.

AND BY WAY OF EXAMPLE
SHE POINTS TO THE SUN

August arrives as a sister horse
whose troubles keep the grass blades quiet.
Erroneous messenger — mind —
many paces haunt the dust. Visible,
but not as a map were they written.
Speechless sun, my arms sway east. I go.

Whose is the voice that tells me to go?
I follow quiet songs like a horse
by whom laws of dusk are written.
The first law is to pass in quiet
all roads as they become visible.
All fields will unfold without the mind

but not as dreams of a larger mind.
No vision, no tree-sigh whispers go.
And so I turn to the visible,
a constellation shaped like a horse
and take my place among the quiet
cities whose profiles will be written

by the moon as rivers are written.
Comprehensible fire of the mind
the animal me enters quiet,
as one figure we will rise to go,
as one daughter, one shadow, one horse.
Solitary door made visible

enters onto barely visible
questions rising off the world, written
as image — a pictographic horse
rendered by the same sapien mind
to ravel this thread, to say we go
as cycles revolving in quiet

harmonics within chaos-quiet.
To the stars we are not visible.
Polaris signals a way to go,
a celestial zero written
as fate's azimuth within the mind.
I will follow, a silent-eyed horse

to pace the quiet spaces written
in visible relations: my mind
holds that those hills have meaning. Go, horse.

ROBERT CREELEY BOARDS
THE S.S. JOHN F. KENNEDY

By a supermarket in Minneapolis
Robert Bly walks with a limp and wild hair to a cafeteria-style
Italian bistro with bottomless glasses of house wine
and silk nosegays that occlude each window.
A banged up Volvo circles the lakes and new parents.
Everybody's pinning their hopes on realism, it's all over the radio.

But nowhere is it broadcast that we lost Robert Creeley
and his blocks of letters, his real letters written in his hand.
When he talked about love
everybody talked about his language, how he said
he would go anywhere for her, like a boat to Staten Island,
a crossword puzzle and news from the entities
traversing his cortex.

On the day he died but not because he died
I decided that love is a decision and not a feeling entirely,
no matter how it ends.
The remainder sits atop a line, not feeling less important
than the whole numbers on the other side of the decimal point.
To answer a question correctly, one must put a noun beside
the number. There is not six, there are six oranges in the sack.
Robert Creeley is dead.
Robert Bly is alive under the same sun and he goes home
to translate a prayer. The young poets write prayers for Creeley
in which he is a photograph of a mountain taped to the wall
above the kitchen sink.

Do not think his poems will sleep in books, books do not sleep.
They just keep arranging papers on your desk,
they keep wishing the lady next to you would stop
eating her chicken like that.

And who needs a bouquet of pussy willows?
Did she go to the city just to buy pussy willows?
You can take a budded wick
into your living room and soon you'll have blossoms,
the limb still thinks it's on the tree.
I am sad to say the word *sad* is a genetically engineered flower
arriving in Odessa, Texas, as we speak.

Go kiss your friends on the mouth, Robert Creeley is dead.
Release the crickets from their cages
of misunderstood musicology, Hart Crane
and Robert Creeley are dead.
The mountain is,
the picture of the mountain is. A poem is never a picture
though it contains many things,
but to name them, what good does that do.

BRIDAL VEIL FALLS

Relax. Relax.
Men climbing cliffs. Relax.

To paint something beautiful is not as good as being
something beautiful.
Relax.

Men climbing cliffs.
In fear and attention you are free from the muttering brain.

Relax.
Your bodies turn to answer the smallest ledges.

You struggle. You will always be too weak.

Relax.

When you prove yourselves to yourselves
you will become avatars

                    of introverted gods.

BRIEF HIST. OF CONTEMP. ART

In the Fifties everyone was wild to capture the atom
of the innermost self, that being a collection of ideas and emotions
and myth approximated in paint. Then the hand, alas,
proved the limits of the body,
not to mention a naked body covered in paint and smeared
against the canvas.
Jim Dine drank a quart of paint then dove through a canvas
and entered the land of the pure idea.
And the next thing we knew, Tuesday was on sale.
People were just shaking hands and that was art.
And so were bad pictures full of ideas.

OH STARS

Even now
under waves
orange fish
flick into flower!

BLUE COAT BESIDE A BLACK JACKET

Whatever composes the incidentals has arranged my days
into a prelude. Not for nothing have you arrived in the instant
the shopkeepers shutter their windows,
dowagers sequester their lapdogs,
and restaurateurs — the relentless aesthetes —
align their potted lemon trees against your entropic questionnaire.

In this moment when, overwhelmed by winter, I abandon words
for pure sight and liken my way through the larger details of April,
spring moves at a thousand-brides-an-hour, the rain enters
an endless state of ending, and brushing my hair becomes
an occasion if it is set to music by a band of ardent carousers
who can think their way through any
amount of wine to leave no virtues unremarked.

Everyone leaves a little space for the one moment
that might change them. Everyone exchanges hellos,
and the kindest among us feeds the rest a few grapes,
a bit of fish if we are lucky. Propose a toast to the open windows,
to us in our audacious charm. Despite ourselves we are all beloved
of someone, none of whom is here tonight.

THIS POEM HAPPENS IN SPRING

It is spring inside the poem and outside the poem.
Inside the poem pageants of tea roses
pose behind a fidgety bride. Her satin heels sink
into the lawn, her bridegroom
swats away an early afternoon cloud
of gnats.
From someplace I don't know yet
a swell of strings arrives — perhaps there's a drive-in
theater nearby and just now a man embraces a woman for vowing
not to board the final flight from their besieged city
without him.
Also inside this poem is a horse that belongs to Franz Marc.
The curves of the grazing horse
lend their shapes to the land and the clouds.
Suppose the clouds shape themselves according
to the shape of a horse.
That would not be love but it would not be unlike love, either.

FAUX TOUGH

The wild youth of Minneapolis consider running the streets
and I lengthen my stride to show I'm down, just not with them.
An emerging leader, the kid in the designer prison pants has tattooed
black scorpions on his arm to signify, perhaps, that he knows
how some killers signify.
It's all the same to the security cameras
that track him and his girlfriend down the cough and cold aisle.
Nobody wants any trouble.
And because she knows the true him and she suggests something
that will work for his congestion and his aches, he puts his hand
in her back pocket.
Some lovers are so discreet and others you have to jack apart
with a rib-spreader — but who are the true lovers?
My affection inches toward you
like a crab asserting itself, then with a wink, withdraws.
A dance to reveal my desire and anticipation
of your immediate departure. Although, if it's all the same to you
I'd like to stop talking now and show you a series
of Japanese woodcuts. See that delicate line?
That's how I want to make you feel.

WHY I LONG TO BE A PINE TREE: GODZILLA'S HAIKU JOURNEY

Midnight

Once again I rise
to gaze upon the city.
Don't know what to eat.

Why I long to be a pine tree

Your guns can't hurt me
not even your laser guns.
Your hate, that hurts me.

We are of an equal grace

Below waves also
I journey through the mountains.
Your moon is my moon.

*The only thing that will stop m*e

Scientists, make me
an underwater plum tree.
Appeal to my heart!

First night of May

You do not know how
I weep like your willow tree
at first sight of spring.

To Kiyoko, princess of the sea

Now I lie down drunk
and count stars instead of fight.
Please be my lady.

To Takashi from Yokohama

Too drunk on plum wine!
Dear crab, don't make me laugh.
Fire shoots out my nose.

Saturday night

Friends, take the journey
to the Brew Thru without me.
Alas, low clearance.

I get so angry sometimes

Tokyo killed Norbu!
Please cut back on the sushi,
the fish are my friends!

Two questions from my exile

People of Tokyo
must you run from me?
Mothra, must we fight?

The end of sunshine

Today I lost a fight.
She won custody of my
little Godzuki!

The Monster's cry

Heart, please stop longing.
No spring beneath the sea
nor winter, nor fall.

Why I must always walk among you

Your war, my mother.
Your atom bomb, my father.
The moon, my flower.

Why I must destroy you

I always told you
the emperor is not god.
Now, you worship me.

THE ARMY OF GOD STRIKES CAMP IN UTAH

There is daily bread and there is surplus.
There is weather and there is the lot we cast.
As the manzanita grove ignores the wind,
so work reveals the spirit of the Christian.
As we are given dominion over all beasts,
so we fashion the deliberate harness.
As men bury the dead,
so women tame fields.
As the mountain is like us but does not know,
so we have sight and do not know.
As children are coaxed to eat,
so God's will is our will,
so we are turned out of our homes,
so we are chosen.

If we were of this world our flaws would have currency
if we were a nation our army could not rest.

YOUR NAME WRITTEN ON A GRAIN OF RICE II

Sunbathers rally to the edge of the breakers to adjust their strings
and wave to their swimmers,
who are too far out but unaware.
Sometimes the ocean lets you read it,
other times it rips you from the shadow of the Hyatt
out to where you hear your name sealed shut
in a fury of galactic nativity.
The physical space reserved for angels dissolves into blue nebulae,
fallopian frills, blurred and winglike.
It is in motion, a manifest light that arrives in unknown frequencies.
Your clean clothes just stay in the basket.
Their insensible presence will dismantle vowel-by-vowel the clouds.

WHAT SHALL I TAKE OF WHAT I NEED?

Fire dominates the clear range of music boxes.
I give them to my Peruvian horse, sad horse that no longer sees
each experience as a Peruvian one. This sun grants
no Peruvian light, nor beach, nor egg,
nor cleaver on a pine plank. He is a lonely horse
and his hoof clops sound like pennies under a blanket.
The plains he'd like to drift toward hold no other horses,
though he does not suspect this.
Together we have walked and walked my land of reconstructed rivers.
It takes me a long time to believe that if I let him go
he will not die or be caught. His father perished on the ocean,
another horseless sky.

SEAWEED THEORY

Grass around, you unkissed trumpets!
The enlisted Color guards of Fortress Monroe
herald evening with a five o'clock cannon.
It turns the starlings west again and startles children
in nightgowns from dream states
above the feverish ant hills.
Heroes, what horses will you water and at what time of day?

Lieutenant, admiral, ensign,
elm and osprey, waxwing above gravel lot,
the Atlantic commences
amid peninsulas and antique artillery.
Tide and brine, each brackish mouth,
an amphibious avenue of invasion.
Phoebus musters her veterans
with myoelectric arms.

Algonquin,
kudzu and creeper, Kecoughtan,
All things beyond ken and control that could harm them they worshipped.
Shipyard apprentice,
my mariner, my Floating Republic,
the union is safe, as sure as time.

Gentle sea star, Saint Mary,
recall how the scallop boats murmured in their slips.
Steam valve, keel and hull, the Chesapeake
once winked and was wise with insular languages.
Beyond that which you have known, your home,
no other emerges.

Fish bones, slave bones, bird bones, English bones,
soldier bones, deer bones,

Powhatan's bones,
sucked-out chicken bones,
house bones, ship bones,
the dug up bones of Statesman Taliaferro.

Poetry of the world illuminated,
a drunken pack of cross-eyed dogs
sniff out my bones, my bones, my bones, my bones.
They survive on nothing.
They advance through pain and fear of death.
Too weak to succeed, they succeed.

Through any engine of searching,
through a new terrain,
at times closer to the sun than others,
add my name to the list
of the infirm or otherwise unreliable.

Homologous structures: wing, hand, and fin.
I have no seaweed theory,
just seaweed intuition.
The fishermen are gone and with them the sea.
Is Virginia my home
if nothing remains to remember me?

FORCES SUSPECTED BUT NEVER OBSERVED

A mermaid rests on my driveway in a puddle.
She was not there before.
She arrived in the night.
What kind of night delivers a mermaid?

What kind of forest swarms with mosses?
Why are cows in the orchards of California?
Beneath the planes of timber are the rings of trees,
beneath my mermaid is a dawn of mirrors.

To move as sunlight through a tidal pool is to excuse a day for ever ending.
It takes her most of the morning to say this.
Her voice is astral wavelength.
At the birthings of stars, every luminous chain of vapors
is a necklace of rock, each necklace, a parade of mermaids.

Quiet star, admit that you delivered the mermaid.
Sudden instant, a puddle can shelter a mermaid. The world
turns wild and gives us fruit.

My neighbor drives by. She works the particle accelerator at CEBAF.
Does she see me talking to a mermaid or talking to a puddle?
Mermaid, get up. If they find you, they'll think
that you mean something. You will indicate a truth
unknown to you. A proof of mermaids.

THE FIRST TIME I SAW THE RIO GRANDE
I COULD ONLY THINK OF MARTY ROBBINS

What they don't tell you if you want to be a singing cowboy is
you will wander from telephone to telephone
and never kiss anyone for real despite your guitar.

You must learn to tell a stranger from a loner
by the length of his stare.

There is a shadow cast by the right way to live.

When you choose a path without prospect, you can buy
what you need with quarters from under the floormat.

Beautiful women with chicken-shit boyfriends are the first to cause
trouble. They pass you their numbers on cocktail napkins
and are not fit for a song
about the lonesome half under lunar influence.

Never take your eyes off your lockbox full of gunfighter ballads.

You must never write a song that ends: *I don't know what I want,*
I don't care, give me anything.

No pasture will receive you after a life of sundown departures.

There is no good or bad but wandering makes it so.

VIRGINS WHO SPEAK IN RIDDLES
WILL NOT STAY VIRGINS LONG

Dolores of the dolorous heart! Dolores with eyeglasses!
With Mexican eyes and a painted house,
how many boys sing in your trees? For you to walk palm to palm,
to speak passively or in riddles,
pour your attention on the Sunday with the big hat.
Tomorrow you will see him here,
and he will see you, but you must keep silent
and sincere as you walk to the fountain
to wash your hands and your nephew's knees.
The house of low infinity, muscles, hotels,
and an animal divide in two.
A voice ordains the palladium dawn.

COMMON DREAM BIRDS

American Crow	Rides thermals in search of splendor, knows human language
Bald Eagle	Raptor that mates in mid air, often seen soaring
Black-crowned Night Heron	Secretive dusk hunter with bright red eye
Brown Creeper	Dark eye below white line, otherwise camouflaged
Brown-headed Cowbird	Infanticidal fledglings, poor parents
Chestnut-sided Warbler	Aspen nest defender, only female incubates
Chimney Swift	Unperched water skimmer, chimney dweller hence name
Common Raven	Unlocker of car doors, oft mistaken for darker self
Dark Eyed Junco	Hierarchical snowwalker, weed eater, chaser of lesser birds
Double-crested Cormorant	Sea crow with unroped wing
Eastern Bluebird	Once thought to bring fortune, now known to auger malice
Eastern Screech Owl	Denizen of the abandoned woodpecker cavity, silent flyer
European Starling	Songster, mimic, causes carwrecks by enchanting commuters
Great Egret	Considered Frenchman of bird world among the French

Hooded Merganser	Wavelet maker, egg abandoner, cohabitater
Killdeer	Most conceptual of birds, fakes injury in vacant fields
Meadowlark	Open-throated grassdiver
Nighthawk	Males fake suicide to woo mates, inhabits urban roofline
Northern Cardinal	Catacretious herald of mid-May, will fight own reflection
Purple Martin	Fully colonized, dwells in human proximities
Red Crossbill	Irruptive spruce seed extractor
Yellow Bellied Sap Sucker	Quiet bird with few vocalizations, will defend sap
Yellow Headed Blackbird	Marsh-singer, perhaps unseeable

LI PO MADE ME THINK

Beside the water lotus all talk of our collective future
did not include separating into teams.

To no fanfare of clouds in the west
pilgrims anointed their troubles intimately.

The merganser seemed to inquire
into a second, more secret night.

By brute immensity or a chirp
we awoke to a white light

arriving through the wicks
of a dreamed-up and blossomless pear tree.

PENNY ARCADE PORTRAIT OF LAUREN BACALL

The memory of it passed through glass
poses as a woman with a whiskey in her hand.
Elixir, chemicals affix the hint
the moon left in your eye.
What words persuaded you to give up your bluff
and were they whispered?
Who knew you shuddered at the delicate stem of iris
aslant in a neck of cut glass?
I surrender too much and ardently
for these times of mine. No one knows the shadows I throw
against the walls of songless alleys
as I gather among the gutter pigeons
cracked watches, milky buttons, dying whispers of starlets,
and a ruined Andromeda fit for the light
of votives. Zeus and Leda,
pucker your lips and blow.

WHAT THINGS DECLARE

      Themselves: a far-off dog,
the radio towers, the small
acacia
holding heat —
traces of past light —
          to its trunk
remind me to declare myself
      a body in this world.

       *

I touch my hand to your arm and I am a thousand lovers.
I bear forward
their thousand gestures in time.

NO ONE CAN ALWAYS EVER
PREDICT CORRECTLY THE WEATHER

Inside of me, an arcade or higher vaulted arches, the interior curve
of an enormous question.
Friend, can you tell me what this is?
Excuse me
while my body takes its natural curve —
the mouth of a shell
asleep on your kitchen floor.

Separate verses of a song rest in the palm of your hand:
four almonds, the length of a sound.
Poorly fed dreams whisper a tunnel through spring,
I was an unkissed mouth beneath a red umbrella
wrecking my sandals in the rain.
And although I was in pain, the pain was not my own,
I was simply in its path, with a few secretaries and a panhandler.

No one could tell me why
I grew so sad each time I saw strangers speaking
to no one but themselves.

Through a cold summer when the hydrangea would not ungreen
my brain embraced a small but artificial window.
Outside, a senile dog that chattered.
I met it with a fist and a faceful of teeth.
The hours grew enormous with sun and rain.
I did not know my work, I did not know my name.
I was invisible despite my burning dress.

Barefoot questions arrived at every four o'clock sunset.
I had a little money.
I was a starving mouthful of smoke.

The haze of a day halved by long sleep
vibrated in my chest slightly faster than a sob.

Without trying I wanted to know every way to draw an apple.
Beakfull by beakfull the cardinal gathered darkness
among the grassleaves.
It sang fragments of song: "Return uncoordinated piano!
Return convalescent brightness!"
Here and there, wild asters.

I demanded a dreamless journey to a mountain fluttered with prayers.
My cheeks took the sun without asking and I offered nothing
but my own death, for which I was not asked.
My friend arrived with a Vallejo poem in which Vallejo arrives
with apples. I felt the absence of a deep embrace
to scale my cobbled well.

Overripe pear uttering its own name,
tell me you're with me on this.

LINES WHISPERED INTO A TEACUP

For two unrecoverable Augusts
I existed as a single shoe in the street.
Each morning the Cambodian handbag vendor
adjusted her hat
so that she could not see me.
Nothing emerged to which I could surrender
though I called for my extinction
in such strange words
the moon revealed to me
its detonated riverbeds,
its blindness.

SPONTANEOUS MONUMENT

On a street clogged with chatter, young men and women
saunter in their casual regalia. I carry the scent of the treeless
suburbs, deliver myself to the ranging antelopes,
the four-story pair of jeans encased in safety glass in case
somebody goes at it with a hammer.
We might think that each other could not resist,
we think that we have never resisted the allure
of an actual response — to see or to be seen and considered,
companioning ourselves to strangers,
imagining for him a sorrow and a memory
of your light-inflected bed.
A shadow pools in the throat of his arm
and your arm lifted to block the sun, these bodies being
engines of song we do not know that we remember.
Your song recalls to me the difference
between the bird and the call of the bird, and how I have failed
to distinguish each act of compassion — an anonymous bouquet
of roses that marks the final embodied moments of someone
who could have been me, I lead myself to believe,
almost ceremonially. Romance abides
in our ideas of death but upon our passing out of memory
the nonaffiliated eavesdroppers shall swarm the cafes, seduced
by the idea that they might belong to anyone — the Japanese one
and the one from New Jersey who jumps when his phone rings.
There are believers
for whom all hopes of an afterlife are buried in code,
as if you could tell by looking
where virtue resides: a woman, all women, a man who crosses
the terrain of his country on foot
and carrying only a proposal of marriage.

In the name of the actual
I have journeyed to the rotunda of the exchange commission
to listen for word of the next round up. Spirited beneath my jacket:
the last indigenous songbird to resist group processing.
There are no minutes revolving parallel to our work
and studied leisures, no monuments to the mind in sandaled feet.
No rest.
I am faithless and in love.

ALL YOU HAVE TO DO IS ASK

Do not drift with the day, little airheaded hunger.
You live four pasts with as many lovers, and each affair ends
with a desire to tender your permission slip
at the entrance of an enchanted universe. Your heart,
like a Vietnamese restaurant, it could be said,
is crammed with magazines and handprinted advertisements
for cleaning services
and lessons in dance and English. Arms recall the weight
of take-out containers, you remember this street from a dream
in which it has balconies
of burnt geraniums and peculiar fish
that live in luminescent trees.
Someone wants to see you if only to mention
your beautiful skin and how the world could meet you differently
if it were just and pleasant
and wept at the sight of its own cherry blossoms
or enlisted the snow to fall on your umbrella.
You might decide it is possible and worthwhile to imagine why
you have come here and why you will leave.
All you have to do is ask and your name will cease to be a word
asleep in a separate bed.
Awaken to a fold in your bedclothes brought to your attention
as though it were an idea, or an error
formed exactly to its purpose.
It is said to live right you must tend to every moment as you would
a stranger afraid of dying. It is not said
that one must struggle, or even take comfort in surviving great peril:
the virtuous vanish utterly and in an instant.
They are not ciphers unless they are.
They observe the world like spies, like watchmen,
like scientists might. For no reason
a little song wells up and it is best whispered to everyone you know.

NOTES

"The Scribe's Umbrella" is for David Shapiro and contains fragments from his lecture, "Two or Three Things I Don't Know about Jasper Johns," delivered at the Walker Art Center, November, 2003.

"It is Interesting and Difficult Work, Ladies" takes its title from a line in *The Age of Anxiety* by W. H. Auden.

"Bridal Veil Falls" begins with three lines by the American painter Paul Thek.

"Penny Arcade Portrait of Lauren Bacall" is the name of a work by the American artist Joseph Cornell.

"No One Can Always Ever Predict Correctly the Weather" takes its title from a quote by the American artist Henry Darger.

The italicized line beginning, *All things beyond ken ...,* in "Seaweed Theory" is from *Tidewater Virginia,* a history by Paul Wilstock, 1929.